Nettie Mugwort the Fairy

Four of these stori_____ ___ ___ _for Nettie,
How Nettie Got her Wings, Nettie's New Shoes
and Nettie's New House — first appeared as
individual picture books. Lynda Britnell has now
added some new stories to make this book.
She lives in Canterbury with her husband, twin
sons and daughter.

Nettie Mugwort the Fairy

Two-minute tales

by Lynda Britnell

Illustrated by Merida Woodford

Dolphin

Published in 2000 as a Dolphin paperback
by Orion Children's Books
a division of the Orion Publishing Group Ltd
Orion House
5 Upper St Martin's Lane
London WC2H 9EA

A catalogue record for this book is available from the British Library

Printed in Great Britain by
The Guernsey Press Co. Ltd, Guernsey, C. I.

ISBN 1 85881 717 X

Contents

A Name for Nettie

One sunny morning a fairy sat under a nettle.

She wasn't an ordinary fairy. She didn't have any wings, she had big feet and she had spiky hair like a hedgehog. And she was very sad because she didn't have a name.

A worm came along the path and stopped by the fairy.

'What's your name?' he asked.

'I don't have a name,' said the fairy.

'Oh dear. Well, Worm is a nice name. We could call you Worm,' said the worm.

'No!' said the fairy. 'I don't want to be called Worm. Worm is not the name for me.'

So the worm went away.

Then a spider came down the path and stopped by the fairy.

'Hello,' said the spider. 'What's your name?'

'I don't have a name,'
said the fairy.

'Oh dear. Well, Spider
is a nice name,' said the
spider. 'We could call you that.'

'No!' said the fairy. 'I don't want
to be called Spider. Spider is not
the name for me.'

So the spider walked on.

Next a caterpillar came down the
path and stopped beside the fairy.

'Hello, what's your
name?' asked the
caterpillar.

'I don't have a
name,' said the fairy.

'Oh dear. Well,
Caterpillar is a nice name. We

could call you Caterpillar,' said the caterpillar.

'No!' said the fairy. 'I don't want to be called Caterpillar. Caterpillar is not the name for me.'

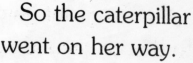

So the caterpillar went on her way.

Finally, a gnome came down the path and stopped beside the fairy.

'You're a new fairy, aren't you?' said the gnome. 'Have you got a name yet?'

'No I haven't,' said the fairy. 'And I don't want to be called Gnome.'

The gnome laughed. 'My name isn't Gnome,' he said. 'It's Know-It-All, and I know how fairies are named. Fairies are named after flowers. Your first name comes from the plant you're found under, and your second name comes from a plant nearby.'

'So what's my name?' said the fairy.

'Well, I found you under these nettles,' said Know-It-All, 'so, your first name is Nettle. And this plant here is mugwort. So your name is Nettle Mugwort.'

'I think,' said Nettle, 'that I would rather be called Nettie Mugwort.'

'Yes,' said Know-It-All, 'I think you are right.'

Nettie danced round and round singing,

'*I am Nettie Mugwort,*
I am Nettie Mugwort,'
until she was quite dizzy.

When she stopped, Know-It-All said, 'We can't leave you here on your own. Come with me and meet the other fairies.'

Know-It-All held Nettie's hand and led her down the path and over a little bridge. Beside the river there were lots of fairies.

'Hello, this is Nettie Mugwort,' said Know-It-All. 'She's a new fairy.'

'Hello, I'm Bluebell,' said a fairy. 'Come and sit with me, Nettie. We're going to have a picnic.'

So Nettie and Know-It-All sat down with Bluebell and the other fairies.

And that is how Nettie Mugwort got her name and came to live in the fairy forest.

How Nettie Got her Wings

Nettie Mugwort was a fairy, but she wasn't an ordinary fairy. She didn't have any wings.

'I wish I had wings like all the other fairies,' said Nettie sadly, 'but where do fairies get their wings from?'

Nettie went to see Mrs Blackbird.

'Mrs Blackbird, where did you get your wings from?' asked Nettie.

Mrs Blackbird opened her wings very wide.

'I didn't get my wings anywhere, Nettie,' she said. 'They just grew.'

Then Nettie went to see Ladybird.

'Ladybird,' she said, 'where did you get your wings from?'

Ladybird flew round very fast and said, 'I didn't get my wings anywhere, they just grew.'

Nettie went home. She looked behind her to see if her wings were growing. She looked and looked, but she couldn't see any wings.

Nettie sat down.

'My wings aren't growing at all,' she thought. 'Where can I get some?'

Just then Nettie's friend Bluebell
peeped round the door.

'Hello, Nettie,' she said. 'What's
wrong?'

Nettie told Bluebell how she
wanted some wings and how she
had asked Mrs Blackbird and
Ladybird where they got theirs.

'But,' said Nettie with a sob, 'they said their wings just grew, and my wings aren't growing at all.'

'Wipe your eyes,' said Bluebell. 'We can get wings at the Spare Wing Shop.'

Nettie wiped her eyes with a big spotted handkerchief and followed Bluebell out of the house, down the path and through the fairy forest.

The Spare Wing Shop was in an old dead tree. Inside the shop there were rows and rows of wings hanging from the ceiling, and boxes of wings piled up everywhere. There was every size from barn owl's wings to gnat's wings.

Nettie tried on
a pair of gnat's
wings, but they
were too small
and when she
tried to fly, only
her heels lifted
off the floor.

19

Next she tried on some beautiful butterfly wings, but they were too big and dragged on the ground.

'These wings are no good,' said Nettie.

So Nettie tried on some bees' wings, and they were just the right size. But bees have four wings, and when she tried to fly with them she flew

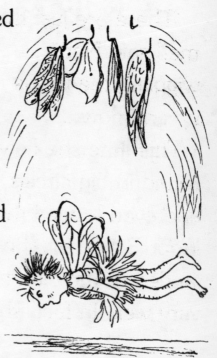

down so low she almost hit the floor.

'Oh dear,' said Nettie. 'I don't think I'll ever find the right wings.'

'Yes, you will,' said Bluebell. 'You need some proper fairy wings.'

Bluebell found some lovely pink wings and Nettie tried them on.

'These are just the wings for me!' said Nettie, wiggling the wings up and down.

This time she flew round in big circles and even looped the loop. But when she landed Nettie didn't feel very well. In fact, she felt sick.

'I don't think I like flying,' said
Nettie, holding her tummy. 'But I
do like the wings.'

So Nettie kept the wings. And
the two friends walked all the way
home.

Nettie and the Egg

Nettie was walking in the forest when she found an egg.

'Oh dear,' said Nettie. 'This egg should be in a nest.'

Nettie carefully rolled the egg to Mrs Blackbird's nest.

'Is this your egg?' she asked.

'No,' said Mrs Blackbird. 'It is
not my egg. My eggs are
speckled, not shiny like that egg.'

Nettie looked at the egg. 'It is
very shiny,' she thought.

Next, Nettie rolled the egg to
Mrs Wren's nest.

'Is this your egg?'
asked Nettie.

'No,' said Mrs
Wren. 'It is not my egg. My eggs
are tiny, but that egg is big.'

Nettie looked at the egg. 'It is
very big,' she thought.

Next, Nettie rolled the egg to
Mrs Starling's nest.

'Is this your egg?' she asked.

'No,' said Mrs Starling. 'It is not

my egg. My eggs are almost
white. That egg is too colourful.'

Nettie looked at the egg. 'It is
very colourful,' she thought. 'And
if no one wants it, I shall sit on it
myself.'

And that is just what she did.
She sat . . .

    and she sat

        . . . and she SAT

on the egg, but nothing happened.

Just then Know-It-All came down the path. He looked at Nettie.

'What are you doing?' asked Know-It-All.

'I am trying to hatch this egg,' said Nettie. 'It's not Mrs

Blackbird's egg because it is too shiny, and it's not Mrs Wren's egg because it's too big, and it's not Mrs Starling's egg because it's too colourful. So I will sit on this egg and hatch it myself.'

'That egg will not hatch,' said Know-It-All. 'Because that is a chocolate egg.'

'A chocolate egg,' said Nettie. 'Are you sure?'

Know-It-All pulled a little of the colourful, shiny paper off the egg and showed Nettie the chocolate shell. Nettie licked her finger and wiped it over the chocolate. It was lovely.

'I think we will roll this egg back

to your house,' said Know-It-All,
'so everyone can have some.'
And that is just what they did.

Nettie's New House

Nettie lived in a hollow log in the forest.

All summer her friends came to visit her there – Know-It-All the gnome, Bluebell the fairy, and Mr Beechtree who owned the sweet shop.

During the day the friends would sit and have tea and honeycakes, and in the evening they would watch the sun go down.

But as summer came to an end the weather got colder. The wind blew leaves and twigs into Nettie's home. The rain blew in and made her mats and chairs wet, and

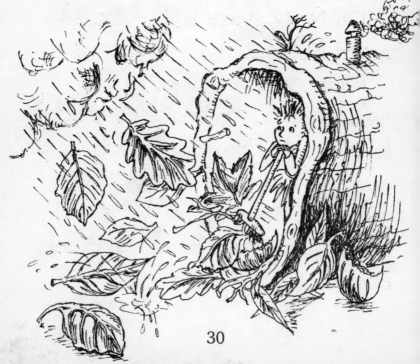

her friends didn't like coming to visit her because it was so cold inside the log.

One morning Bluebell came to see Nettie.

'Good morning, Nettie,' said Bluebell, but Nettie didn't answer. She was sitting in a chair holding a cup of tea and sniffing loudly.

'Oh Nettie, what is the matter?' asked Bluebell.

'I don't feel well,' said Nettie, rubbing her red nose. 'All night long it rained and the wind blew and now I've got a horrible cold.'

'We will have to find you a new warm home,' said Bluebell. 'Come along.'

So Nettie and Bluebell went off to find Nettie a new home.

The town was full of toadstool houses.

Some were small with flat tops.

Some were middle-sized with domed tops.

Some were large with spotted tops.

Nettie stood beside a small flat-topped toadstool.

'This is no good,' said Nettie. 'I'm taller than the roof of this house.'

Then Nettie and Bluebell went
to see a middle-sized toadstool
with a domed roof.

'This is bigger,' said Bluebell.
'Yes, it is,' said Nettie, 'but I will
have to crawl through the front
door. It is still not big enough.'
Next they went to a large
toadstool with a high spotted roof.

'This will be big enough,' said Bluebell.

Nettie could just get through the door but when she tried to stand straight up inside the toadstool . . . **BOMP!** She hit her head on the ceiling.

'Oh dear,' said Bluebell. 'We don't have any bigger toadstools. Where are you going to live?'

The two friends walked sadly to Mr Beechtree's sweet shop. Bluebell told Mr Beechtree how all the toadstools were too small.

'Have you looked at the old oak tree across the path?' said Mr Beechtree. 'No one has lived there for a long time because it is too big.'

Nettie, Bluebell and Mr Beechtree hurried to the old oak tree.

Mr Beechtree pushed open the door. The doorway was much bigger than Nettie, so she didn't have to crawl in. And the ceiling was much higher, so she didn't bang her head. Nettie looked around and smiled.

'This will be my new home,' she said.

Know-It-All, Bluebell and Mr Beechtree all helped Nettie carry her table and chairs, her plates and cups and her bed into the old oak tree.

When they had put everything safely in her new home, Nettie

and her friends had a lovely tea of lemonade and honeycakes.

And Nettie Mugwort has lived in the old oak tree ever since.

Nettie and the Birthday Cake

It was Bluebell's birthday.

Bluebell was Nettie's best friend, so Nettie wanted to get a very special present for her. She sat and thought about what she could get Bluebell.

'I could get her some ribbons for her hair,' thought Nettie. 'But she has lots of ribbons already.'

She thought some more.

'I could get her a nice warm scarf,'

thought Nettie. 'But she has a lovely stripy one already. What would Bluebell like?'

Nettie jumped up.

'I know what Bluebell would like!' she cried. 'I will make her a birthday cake. A chocolate birthday cake, because Bluebell loves chocolate.'

Nettie found the recipe for chocolate cake. Then she went to the cupboard and got out everything she needed to make the cake.

The flour and the baking powder.

The margarine and sugar.

Two eggs.

And a tablespoon
of cocoa powder.
Nettie put all
the ingredients
into a big bowl
and mixed them
all together.

Then she put the mixture in two round tins and put them in the oven to cook.

After a while, Nettie thought, 'I will just open the oven door to see if they are cooked.'

She opened the oven door and peeped inside.

The cakes were getting taller. Nettie was very pleased.

But as she looked . . . the cakes began to sink!

Nettie quickly shut the oven door again.

When it was time for the cakes to come out of the oven, she opened the door wide.

There inside the oven were two flat cakes!

'Oh dear,' said Nettie. 'I will have to make the cakes again. But this time I won't open the oven door too soon.'

So Nettie got out all the
ingredients for the cake again.

The flour and the baking powder.

The margarine.

Two more eggs.

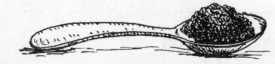

And a spoonful of cocoa powder.

Nettie got out her big bowl and mixed everything together. She put the mixture into two cake tins and put them in the oven.

But this time Nettie DIDN'T open the oven door.

When it was time to get the cakes out of the oven, they were nice and big. Nettie put them on a tray to cool.

A little piece of cake fell off, so Nettie tasted it. It wasn't very nice, so she tried another piece.

'Yuk!' said Nettie. 'This cake doesn't taste sweet at all.'

Nettie thought about how she had made the cake.

'I put in the flour and the baking

powder. I put in the margarine
and the eggs and the spoonful of
cocoa powder. Why doesn't the
cake taste sweet?'

Then Nettie said, 'Oh no! I
forgot to put in the sugar!'

So for the third time Nettie put
all the ingredients in her big bowl.

She put it in the two round cake
tins and popped them in the oven.

This time the cake came out just
right.

Nettie fixed the two halves
together with jam and put lots of
candles on top.

'Thank you, Nettie,' said
Bluebell. 'You must be very clever
to make a cake like that.'

'Not really,' said Nettie. But she thought to herself, 'I do try hard.'

Nettie's New Shoes

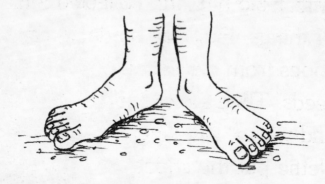

Nettie had big feet. They were bigger than an ordinary fairy's feet. In fact, Nettie's feet were three times bigger than an ordinary fairy's feet. And this was a problem, because none of the shoe shops had shoes in Nettie's size. All the shoes she tried on were too small.

So Nettie thought, 'I will make my own shoes.'

She went into the fairy forest with a big bag and collected lots of things. First she made some shoes from dandelion seeds. They looked soft and warm. But when Nettie put the shoes on, sand got in them and tickled her toes.

Next she made some shoes from sweet chestnut shells. They wouldn't let the sand in to tickle her toes. But when Nettie put them on she prickled her fingers.

'Ouch!' she said. 'If I trod on someone I would hurt them.'

Last of all Nettie made some shoes from moss. They wouldn't hurt if she trod on someone.

But when she walked out in the rain the moss got soggy and Nettie's feet got wet.

Nettie sat down. 'Oh, what shall I do?' she said.

But then she heard a

thump! thump! thump!

It was coming closer.

Thump! thump! thump!

And closer:

THUMP!

THUMP!

THUMP!

And closer:

THUMP!

        THUMP!

                THUMP!

Out of the trees came Know-It-All the Gnome. He stopped beside Nettie.

'What's wrong?' he said.

Nettie told him about her problem feet and how she couldn't find any shoes to fit.

'Your feet aren't a problem,' said Know-It-All. 'Come with me.'

And that is what she did.

Know-It-All took her to a shop called Gnome Your Feet. Gnome Your Feet was a wonderful place. There were all kinds of shoes:

big shoes

and little shoes,

plain shoes

and sparkly shoes.

Nettie found a pair of pink
hiking boots that fitted perfectly.

'They may not be as small as
other fairies' shoes,' said Nettie.
'But they fit,' said Know-It-All.
'And I like them,' said Nettie.

Nettie and the Pot of Gold

One morning, Nettie was walking in the woods. She had just jumped over the little stream when it started to rain.

'Oh dear,' said Nettie. 'I hope it isn't going to rain hard or I will get very wet!'

She looked up at the sky. There were a few small grey clouds above her. But just then the sun began to shine.

'How strange,' said Nettie. 'It's rainy and sunny at the same time.'

'No,' said Frog. 'I've been sitting here all morning, but I haven't seen the end of the rainbow or a pot of gold.'

'Oh bother,' said Nettie. 'I was sure the end of the rainbow was here.' She looked up at the sky again. 'I think the end must be in the woods. I wonder if Squirrel has found the gold.'

And with that she ran off towards the woods.

By the time she reached the woods Nettie was out of breath again. She looked behind the trees and in the bushes for the end of the rainbow, but she couldn't see it anywhere.

Just then she saw Squirrel sitting up on a branch chewing a nut.

'Hello, Squirrel,' called Nettie. 'Have you found the pot of gold at the end of the rainbow?'

'No,' said Squirrel. 'I've been sitting in these branches all morning but I haven't seen the end of the rainbow or a pot of gold.'

'Oh bother,' said Nettie. 'I was sure the end of the rainbow was here!'

She looked at the rainbow
again. 'I know where it ends!' she
cried. And she started to run
towards Bluebell's house. Just as
she got there . . . the rainbow
seemed to move away.

'Well, I'm blowed!' said Nettie.
'It looks as if the rainbow is
finishing up at my house!'

So without stopping she ran
home as fast as she could.

By the time she got there, Nettie was very tired indeed and the end of the rainbow was nowhere to be seen. In fact, the rainbow had completely disappeared.

'Oh, well,' said Nettie. 'Perhaps I'll find it next time.'

Then she noticed a big pot standing beside her front door. Nettie ran to look inside it.

It was a huge jar of golden honey.

'Maybe I did find the end of the rainbow after all,' said Nettie.

And she picked up the honey and went inside to have her lunch.

Nettie's Flower Patch

Nettie was reading the newspaper.
It said:

Nettie thought, 'This is the job for me. I will go to the Flower School.'

So she combed her spiky hair, cleaned her teeth, put on her pink boots, and set off to the Fairy Flower School.

The teacher at the school sat behind a big desk.

'Are you sure you're a fairy?' asked the teacher. 'It's just that you have spiky hair, and you are very tall, and you wear pink boots.'

'Yes, I am a fairy,' said Nettie, 'and I will be good at looking after flowers.'

Nettie went to the school all week.

On Monday she learnt about seeds and how to plant them.

On Tuesday she learnt about

what a seed needed to grow . . .
sunshine,

rain

and care.

On Wednesday Nettie learnt that you mustn't have the flowers too close together or they won't grow.

On Thursday
she learnt how
insects use flowers
for food . . .

bees . . .

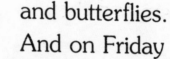

and butterflies.
And on Friday
Nettie learnt how
to gather the
seeds when the
flowers die, to use
again next year.
Back home
Nettie planted her
seeds, and waited
for them to grow.

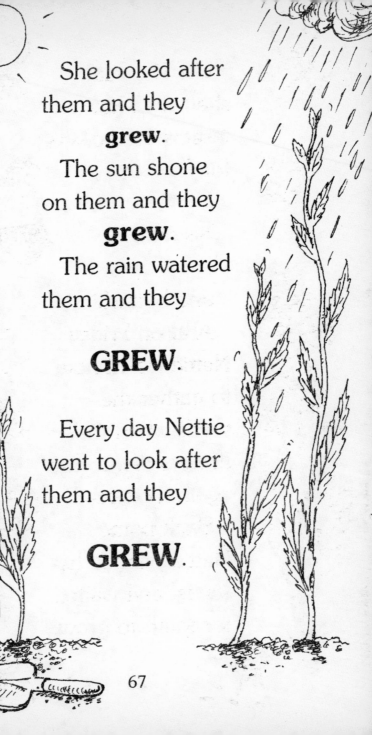

She looked after
them and they
grew.
The sun shone
on them and they
grew.
The rain watered
them and they

GREW.

Every day Nettie
went to look after
them and they

GREW.

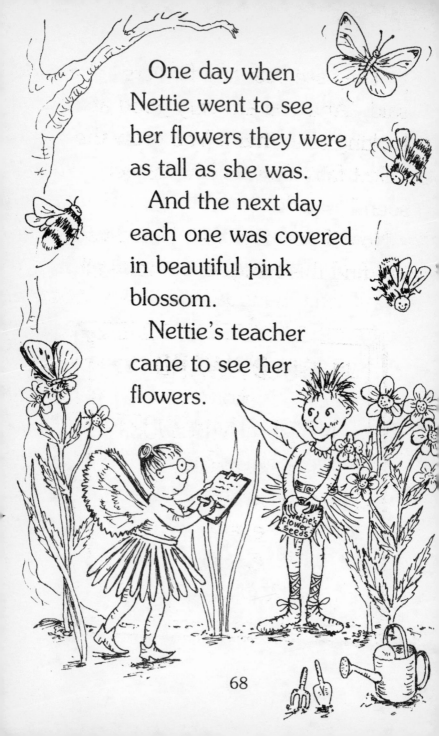

One day when Nettie went to see her flowers they were as tall as she was.

And the next day each one was covered in beautiful pink blossom.

Nettie's teacher came to see her flowers.

68

'They are beautiful flowers,' she said. 'And you are very good at looking after them. You grow the tallest fairy flowers I have ever seen.'

Now if you ever visit Nettie you will find this hanging on her wall:

☆ **GOLD AWARD** ☆
to
NETTIE MUGWORT
for growing
the tallest fairy flowers
<u>ever</u>!
Signed: *Rose Bay*
ROSE BAY (TEACHER)
FAIRY FLOWER SCHOOL.

Nettie and the Summer Fair

It was summer. The fairies were getting ready for the summer fair.

Nettie and Bluebell had painted a maypole and fixed brightly coloured ribbons to the top. Know-It-All had shown some of the fairies how to dance round the maypole.

As they danced the ribbons wove a colourful pattern.

'It looks very pretty,' thought Nettie. 'But we need some music to dance to. Where can I find some music?'

Nettie walked into the forest and
listened.

She could hear the wind blowing
in the trees. It made a rustling
sound.

'The wind sounds very nice,'
said Nettie. 'But it isn't music.'

Then Nettie went to the river.

The water was tumbling over the stones, making a babbling sound.

'The river sounds very nice too,' said Nettie. 'But that isn't music either.'

Nettie walked into the meadow and sat down. 'Oh, where can I find some music?' she said.

Just then she heard a whistling sound.

'That sounds like music,' said Nettie, and she jumped up and followed it.

As she walked across the meadow the music grew louder.

'I wonder who's playing it,' she thought. The music was very loud now, but she still couldn't see anyone.

Netttie looked around. There was no one there. All she could see was the grasses blowing in the wind.

But when the wind stopped
blowing, the music stopped too.

'The wind's playing the music
on the grass,' said Nettie.

So she went and blew on a
hollow piece of grass. It made a
whistle.

Then Nettie blew on another
piece of grass.

It made a different whistle.

Soon she had tried six different grasses. Each one made a different whistle.

'I will take these home and learn to play music,' thought Nettie. So she collected up the grasses and started to walk home.

She was walking down the path when she heard a rattling noise.

'That sounds nice,' she thought. She followed the noise to a hedge. There she found some old poppy seed heads. When the wind blew, they made a rattling sounds.

'I will take them home too,'
said Nettie.

Just then she saw Bluebell.

'What are you doing, Nettie?'
asked Bluebell.

'I'm going to make music,'
said Nettie. And she told
Bluebell all about it.

Nettie and Bluebell were
almost home when they
heard a strange noise. The
two friends followed it till
they came to a big tree.

Every time the wind blew,
a loose piece of bark hit the
side of the tree and made a
tapping sound.

'That's nice,' said Nettie.

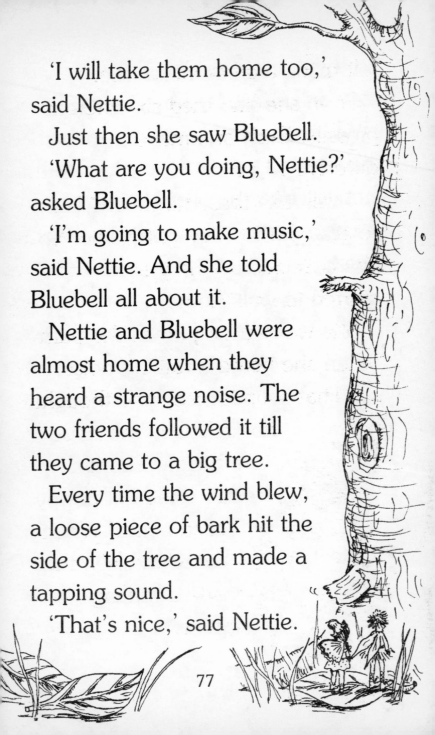

So they picked up the piece of
bark and carried it home.

When they got home Nettie tied
the six pieces of grass together with
string. Then she blew them . . .

They made a beautiful whistling
noise.

Bluebell dusted the old poppy
seed heads and held one in each
hand.

Then she shook them . . .
They made a rattling sound.

Next Nettie and Bluebell cut the
bark into different sized pieces.
Nettie hit each one with a spoon . . .
They made a tapping sound.

By the summer fair, Nettie's Band was ready. Mr Beechtree played the bark, Bluebell played the poppy seed heads and Nettie played the grasses.

And while the fairies danced round the maypole - the whole forest rang with Nettie's music!

Nettie's Harvest

It was harvest time. The fairies were busy gathering in the fruit and vegetables to store away for the winter. Nettie was putting seeds into sacks ready to be planted in the spring.

When she had finished, Nettie
went to find her friend Bluebell.

Bluebell and some other fairies
were by a big blackberry bush.
They had been picking
blackberries all day, and now the
bushes were almost bare. Bluebell
was flying above the bush, picking
the last berries from the very top

and putting them carefully in the baskets.

Nettie looked through the leaves into the middle of the bush. In there she saw lots of big, ripe blackberries.

'Are you going to pick those too?' asked Nettie.

'Oh no,' said Bluebell. 'We can't pick those. If we crawl into the bush, the thorns will catch our wings and tear them.'

'I can take off my wings,' said Nettie, 'and crawl in and get them.'

And with that, Nettie took off her wings and laid them gently on the grass.

'Be careful,' warned Bluebell, as Nettie started to crawl into the bush. 'The thorns are very sharp.'

Nettie started to pick some berries, but as she tried to crawl further in the thorns caught on her clothes and in her hair.

'It's no good,' she thought. 'I must find something to help me make a pathway in.'

Nettie crawled back out of the bush and the two friends walked off along the hedgerow looking for something that could help them get to the blackberries.

They had not walked far when Nettie saw a large pile of sticks.

She picked up one of the sticks and looked at it. It was very long and straight with a hooked piece on the end.

Nettie had an idea.

'Let's collect all the sticks like this one,' she said to Bluebell.

'All right,' said Bluebell.
When they each had an
armful of sticks they
carried them
back to the
blackberry
bush.

All the fairies
watched as
Nettie took a stick
and crawled into the bush.

When she was inside, she caught
a thorny branch with the hook at
the end of her stick. She pulled the
branch to one side and pushed the
stick into the ground. Then she
got another stick and did the same
again, then another, then another.

Soon the way into the bush was clear.

'Look!' cried Bluebell. 'Nettie has made a tunnel into the blackberry bush!'

All the fairies clapped and cheered as Nettie gathered the big, juicy blackberries and passed them out to Bluebell.

When all the berries were picked, Nettie crawled out of the bush, collecting all the sticks as she came.

'Oh Nettie,' said Bluebell, 'that was a clever idea.'

And from then on the fairies always used Nettie's blackberry sticks at harvest time.

Nettie and the Cold Day

A cold wind blew. Nettie Mugwort opened her front door and looked out.

'Oh, it's cold!' she said. 'I will have to put on warm clothes.' And she went back inside.

'Now, what
can I wear?'
thought Nettie.
'I can wear my
warm coat . . .

 and my warm
hat . . .

and my warm
mittens.'
She put them on.

'Now I can go out in the cold,' said Nettie.

Out in the wood the cold wind was blowing very hard.

Nettie went to see her friend Tree. But Tree wasn't very well. All his leaves were blowing off.

'Oh dear,' said Nettie. 'Tree is ill.
I must help him.'

She ran home to fetch some
glue,

her sewing box,

a hammer

and some nails.

By the time she got back to Tree,
more of his leaves had fallen off.

Nettie set to work. First she put all the fallen leaves in a big pile. Then she got out her hammer and nails. She tried to nail a leaf back on one of Tree's branches, but the branch was too thin and Nettie hit her thumb instead.

Next she got out her glue. She painted the glue on Tree's branches and started to stick the leaves back on. But the wind blew them off before they could stick, and they just stuck to Nettie. One leaf stuck on her nose.

So Nettie opened
her sewing box and
took out her needle
and thread.

She tried to sew the
leaves on Tree, but
the branches were too
hard and her needle bent.

'What am I to do?' thought
Nettie. 'I can't nail the leaves to
Tree. I can't glue the leaves to
Tree. I can't sew the leaves on
Tree. How can I make him well?'

Just then Nettie saw Know-It-All.

She told Know-It-All that Tree
was ill and that his leaves kept
falling off and how she had tried
to help.

'But Nettie, Tree isn't ill,' said Know-It-All. 'Winter is coming. Tree's leaves fall off and Tree goes to sleep until spring. It happens every year.'

'Oh, so Tree is getting ready for bed!' said Nettie. 'Perhaps I should make him a big spotted nightdress!'

'Oh, Nettie, you are funny!' laughed Know-It-All.

Nettie smiled and the two faries hurried home through the wood.